A LITTLE GUIDE TO
TO
BUBBLE TEA

T0364079

RP Minis®
Hachette Book Group
1290 Avenue of the Americas, New York, NY 10104
www.runningpress.com
@Running_Press

First Edition: May 2023

Published by RP Minis, an imprint of Perseus Books, LLC, a subsidiary of Hachette Book Group, Inc. The RP Minis name and logo is a registered trademark of the Hachette Book Group.

The publisher is not responsible for websites (or their content) that are not owned by the publisher.

ISBN: 978-0-7624-8356-3

CONTENTS

INTRO-DUCTION

SIP SIP HOORAY!

We're here to celebrate a pop idol, an international sensation with legions of devoted followers. If you think this crowd-pleaser is a musician, then we're sorry to burst your *bubble*. We're not talking about pop music. We're talking about the *pop of* a tapioca pearl between your teeth. We're talking about the oddly satisfying *pop* of an oversized straw piercing a plastic film seal. We are, of course, talking about the *pop* culture phenomenon that is bubble tea!

In its simplest form, bubble tea is a cold drink that contains chewy tapioca balls. It's also known as boba tea or pearl milk. No matter what you call it, this beloved beverage is as delicious as it is Instagrammable. Its colorful aesthetic makes it the ultimate viral drink—but unlike other foodie fads and

#trends, bubble tea is here to stay. And unlike some cash-grab seasonal offerings, it's there for you all year round. (Pumpkin spice lattes and Shamrock Shakes could never!)

So where did this drink come from? How did it become so popular? Why is it so cool, both temperature- and clout-wise? It's time to spill the tea . . . about bubble tea!

A BRIEF HISTORY OF BOBA

Like all great legends, the origins of bubble tea are a little mysterious and often disputed. There isn't a definitive, singular way to explain something so exquisite. What we do know is that bubble tea originated in Taiwan in the late 1980s. Milk tea was already popular in East Asia, and chewy tapioca balls were commonly used in desserts. Taiwanese teahouses started to combine the two treats, and the rest is history.

You might think the "bubble" in bubble tea refers to those glorious globs of tapioca starch. The word is actually a reference to the bubbly layer of foam that appears when you shake or stir the drink. "Boba" is the name of the tapioca pearls, as well as the drink itself. The word is also Chinese slang for big breasts! (Pro tip: If you're in a Chinese-speaking country and you on't want to order boobs, you can say *hēn zhū*, which means "pearls.")

From these humble (and buxom) beginnings, boba shops started popping up across Southeast Asia and became a cultural craze among trendy youth. Bubble tea eventually made its way to the United States in the late 1990s, thanks to entrepreneurial Taiwanese Americans who opened the first boba shops in California. The state-wide debut of boba dovetailed with the rise of café culture and blended ice drinks from places like Starbucks in the

late '90s and early 2000s. It wasn't lon
before social media drove this trend
tea into neighboods and newsfeed
all over the world.

Part of the joy of boba comes fror
its versatility. It's a creamy beverag
and a chewy snack all at once. Ther
are countless flavors and combos tha
allow you to have your boba any wa
you like. You can make it milky or fruit
(or both!), and you can switch out th
pearls for jellies and other mix-ins. Wit
so many different ways to customiz
bubble tea, the world is your boba!

POPULAR BUBBLE TEA FLAVORS

CLASSIC MILK TEA

Bubble tea has evolved into many different flavors and styles, each more experimental than the last. But this classic combo is the one that started it all. It combines freshly brewed black tea with milk, crushed ice, and tapioca pearls. The pearls are made by rolling tapioca starch into bite-size balls, which are then boiled. Since tapioca has a neutral taste, the balls are typically flavored with sugar or honey to create a caramelized confection. The result is a creamy, sweet drink that is cool and refreshing. Classic milk tea is the original and arguably the best.

TARO

Taro is a starchy root vegetable similar to yam. It has been a staple food in the Pacific Islands for thousands of years and is a popular ingredient in many Asian dishes. Although taro bubble tea has a distinctly lavender lewk, the tasty tuber has mostly white flesh

with small specks of purple. The pretty pastel hue of taro boba typically comes from food coloring, which is added when manufacturers process taro into a powder. Many bubble tea shops use taro powder rather than fresh taro for this reason. Real taro boba will have a much more subtle pinkish-white color. Whether powdered or fresh, taro remains one of the most popular bubble tea flavors.

MATCHA

Matcha is a finely ground powder made from green tea leaves. Green tea is typically made by steeping leaves in hot water—once the flavor infuses into the liquid, you discard the leaves. With matcha, you consume the actual leaves that have been stone-ground into a fine powder. The powder is whisked into hot water with a bamboo brush to create a frothy solution. This traditional method of preparation dates back to 12th-century China and Japan. In the 21st century, matcha has become a popular base for bubble tea. The deep, earthy flavor combines with the sweetened pearls to create a matcha made in heaven!

STRABERRY

The simple pairing of strawberries and cream is thought to have been introduced at a banquet for Henry VIII in 1509. The dessert became fashionable in 19th-century England, where it was considered the height of sophistication. In a time before refrigeration,

the seasonal berries were only available for a few weeks every year, so eating them was a luxury. These days, you don't have to be royalty to enjoy the luxurious royal-tea of strawberry boba! Strawberry-flavored milk is served over chewy tapioca pearls to create a pretty-in-pink beverage. In many bubble tea shops, the beverage does not actually contain tea at all. Even if your strawberry milk tea is more of a strawberry milk drink, it will hit the spot.

THAI

On the streets of Bangkok and elsewhere in Thailand, iced tea is a popular drink that is perfect for the country's hot climate. Thai iced tea is called *cha yen*, which translates to "cold tea." Strong black tea is often brewed with ingredients like orange blossom water, star anise, tamarind, and other spices. Rather than using fresh milk, the tea is made with evaporated milk, condensed milk, or a creamy blend of both. This creates a very sweet beverage with a smooth texture that pairs beautifully with boba. Thai bubble tea has a striking orange color that sets it apart from beige milk teas. Orange is the new black—or, in this case, milk—tea!

BROWN SUGAR

This indulgent beverage is also known as tiger milk tea because of the caramel tiger stripes that streak the inside of the cup. The central ingredient is brown sugar syrup, which imbues fresh cold milk with a rich sweetness. When this flavor launched in Taiwanese shops

in 2017, people lined up for hours to get a taste. If you're doing it for the 'gram, be sure to take your picture immediately because the stripes will dissolve within a few minutes. Once you've posted your pic (no filter required for this boba beauty!), shake or stir it all up and enjoy your swirling sugary drink.

MANGO

If you want a tropical refresher, look no further than mango bubble tea. Sweet, juicy mango puree is poured over tapioca pearls to create this drink. It typically doesn't contain actual tea, but it can be blended with green tea if you're feeling particularly thirst-tea.

The mango flavor can also be included in special pearls called popping boba. These balls are not made from tapioca, but instead have juice inside a thin, gel-like membrane. When this skin is pierced between your teeth, the fruit flavor bursts with a satisfying pop. If ASMR were a beverage, it would be a bubble tea with popping boba.

WINTER MELON

Winter melon bubble tea is light and fresh with a delicate, mild taste. The melon itself is a large oblong fruit that is closely related to cucumber and zucchini. It is a staple in Asian cuisine, often featured in soup and stir-fry, and is also used in Eastern medicine.

For bubble tea, the melon is cooked with sugar to create a syrup or blended paste. When this is combined with tea, milk, and boba, the subtle flavor creates a refreshing drink that is perfect for a hot summer day, whether you're in Singapore, Shanghai, or San Francisco.

WHAT'S YOUR BUBBLE TEA?

NOW YOU KNOW THE GREATEST HITS OF BOBA, BUT DO YOU KNOW YOUR BOBA STYLE?

TAKE THIS TASTE TEST TO FIND THE FLAVOR THAT BEST SUITS YOU!

What is your favorite season?

- **A** Fall (crisp and cool)
- **B** Winter (cozy and snuggly)
- **C** Summer (fun in the sun)
- **D** Spring (fresh new beginnings)

Pick your next vacation.

- **A** A long weekend in Paris
- **B** Luxury spa in Dubai
- **C** Clubbing in Ibiza
- **D** An eco-friendly resort in Tulum

How do you start your day?

A A routine of stretching and making a simple breakfast

B Hitting snooze and sleeping in

C Scrolling through social media

D Journaling and saying affirmations

Which style of music do you prefer?

A. Contemporary classics and greatest hits

B. Smooth jazz

C. Anything that makes you dance

D. Meditation music and nature sounds

What emoji do you use most?

A Thumbs up

B Winking face

C Party cone

D Yoga pose

You're craving a snack. What would you like?

A Granola bar

B Chocolate truffles

C A bag of Pop Rocks

D Celery and carrot sticks

What is your dream home?

A Craftsman house with a wraparound porch

B Decadent mansion

C Penthouse apartment

D Beach bungalow

What is something you never leave home without?

A Wallet, phone, keys

B Designer bag

C A can of Red Bull

D Healing crystals

What makes you cringe most?

- **A** Secondhand embarrassment
- **B** Penny pinchers
- **C** Leaving the party first
- **D** People who litter

Which shoes will you wear today?

- **A** Comfortable sneakers
- **B** Prada loafers
- **C** Sparkly boots
- **D** Open-toed sandals

If you answered mostly As, you're classic cool. You thrive on routine and enjoy the simple things in life. Keep things traditional with a classic milk tea or taro bubble tea.

If you answered mostly Bs, you're a sweet tooth. You like to indulge and have zero guilt about guilty pleasures. Enjoy a rich cup of brown sugar boba or Thai milk tea.

If you answered mostly Cs, you're fruity fun. You're the life of the party! Order something that's as bright and joyful as you are: strawberry or mango bubble tea.

If you answered mostly Ds, you're **clean and conscious**. You love wellness and clean living, so you already know the health benefits of matcha and winter melon. Why not choose one as the base for your next bubble tea?

This book has been bound using handcraft methods and Smyth-sewn to ensure durability.

The dust jacket and interior were illustrated by Sol Cotti and designed by Justine Kelley.

The text was written by Melissa Maxwell.